Facts About the Ocelot

By Lisa Strattin

© 2019 Lisa Strattin

FREE BOOK

FREE FOR ALL SUBSCRIBERS

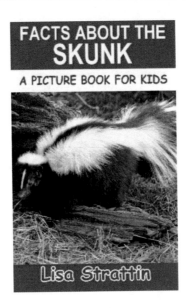

LisaStrattin.com/Subscribe-Here

BOX SET

- **FACTS ABOUT THE POISON DART FROGS**
- **FACTS ABOUT THE THREE TOED SLOTH**
- **FACTS ABOUT THE RED PANDA**
- **FACTS ABOUT THE SEAHORSE**
- **FACTS ABOUT THE PLATYPUS**
- **FACTS ABOUT THE REINDEER**
- **FACTS ABOUT THE PANTHER**
- **FACTS ABOUT THE SIBERIAN HUSKY**

LisaStrattin.com/BookBundle

Facts for Kids Picture Books by Lisa Strattin

Little Blue Penguin, Vol 92

Chipmunk, Vol 5

Frilled Lizard, Vol 39

Blue and Gold Macaw, Vol 13

Poison Dart Frogs, Vol 50

Blue Tarantula, Vol 115

African Elephants, Vol 8

Amur Leopard, Vol 89

Sabre Tooth Tiger, Vol 167

Baboon, Vol 174

Sign Up for New Release Emails Here

LisaStrattin.com/subscribe-here

COVER IMAGE

https://www.flickr.com/photos/martyn404/5181637389/

ADDITIONAL IMAGES

https://www.flickr.com/photos/skrewtape/2436007178/

https://www.flickr.com/photos/15016964@N02/5661940917/

https://www.flickr.com/photos/43555660@N00/16233413356/

https://www.flickr.com/photos/ekilby/4806231977/

https://www.flickr.com/photos/jitze1942/14057302822/

https://www.flickr.com/photos/atul666/4530109039/

https://www.flickr.com/photos/jitze1942/16695676584/

https://www.flickr.com/photos/jitze1942/17130572510/

https://www.flickr.com/photos/becker271/3657408536/

https://www.flickr.com/photos/martyn404/5181637389/

Contents

INTRODUCTION

the Ocelot is a medium-sized small cat that lives in the South American jungles, as well as a few other select places. They are also called Painted Leopards because the markings on their fur is distinctive with spots and stripes. They are closely related to the Margay. They climb and run well, as well as being very good swimmers.

BEHAVIOR

The Ocelot has a home range of up to 11.5 square miles, depending on the area where they live. Males like to patrol the home territory to make sure no other Ocelots are moving in! Normally they sleep during the day on a branch or in thick vegetation on the ground. They do most of their hunting at night.

APPEARANCE

The Ocelot has thick, short, velvety fur that is a tawny-yellow to a reddish-grey color. They have black markings on their back and sides. There are also stripes on their head and face as well as dark spots on their head. Their tail has dark rings on it. Overall, the Ocelot looks just like a pretty housecat, just a bit bigger!

REPRODUCTION

The Ocelot breeds all year round. After mating the female will find a hollow place in the rocks around where she lives to make a place to have her babies. She is pregnant for almost 3 months and usually has a litter of only 2 or 3 kittens. The kittens fur is dark when they are born and the colors become more evident when they are about 4 weeks old. They are full grown at about 1 year of age and will usually leave the mother's home range shortly after that to determine their own territory.

LIFE SPAN

Ocelots live for 8 to 12 years, on average.

SIZE

The adult Ocelot is 22 to 40 inches long and weighs 25 to 35 pounds. This is about twice the average weight of most housecats.

HABITAT

Most Ocelots live in the jungles of South America. Although they have been spotted as far north as the very southern areas of Texas! They can live in grasslands, forests, mangroves and marshes, as long as there is plenty of vegetation for them to hide in, they seem to do well in many different types of habitats. Since they are strong swimmers, even occasional flooding does not pose much of a problem for them.

DIET

Ocelots are meat eaters that sleep or rest during the day and hunt at night, They eat a lot of rodents, but also like rabbits, fish, birds, lizards and crabs. They have been known to eat snakes too. Of larger animals, they will hunt and eat monkeys, armadillos, anteaters and turtles. For the most part, any small to medium-sized animal that is part of their native range is a possible meal for them.

ENEMIES

Ocelots do have several enemies in their natural range. Larger cats like the Jaguars and Pumas will hunt and kill them, as well as the Harpy Eagle, the Anaconda Snake and large Birds of Prey. The coloring of the Ocelot helps them to maintain cover of camouflage much of the time.

SUITABILITY AS PETS

Believe it or not, the Ocelot has been kept as a pet throughout history. It's probably not a pet for everyone, but they have been successfully tamed to the point that people have made them a pet. In some areas they might be illegal to keep, but, if not, you likely need a special permit. So be sure to check your local laws before deciding that you want one!

Bear in mind, though, that the Ocelot is a wild animal and needs meat to thrive, so it's not a house pet that you could feed cat food from your local pet store. it's probably a better idea for you to see some at your local zoo, instead of getting one for a pet.

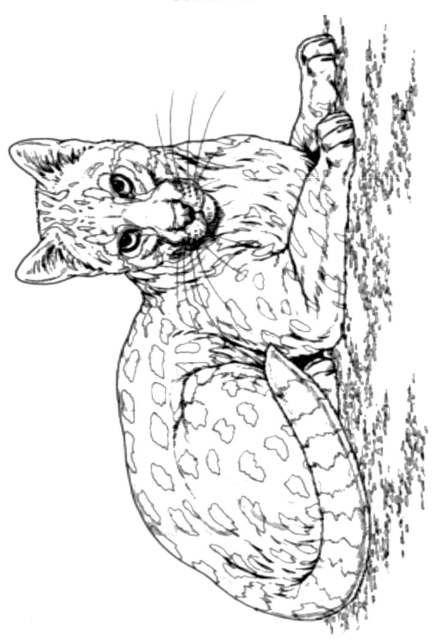

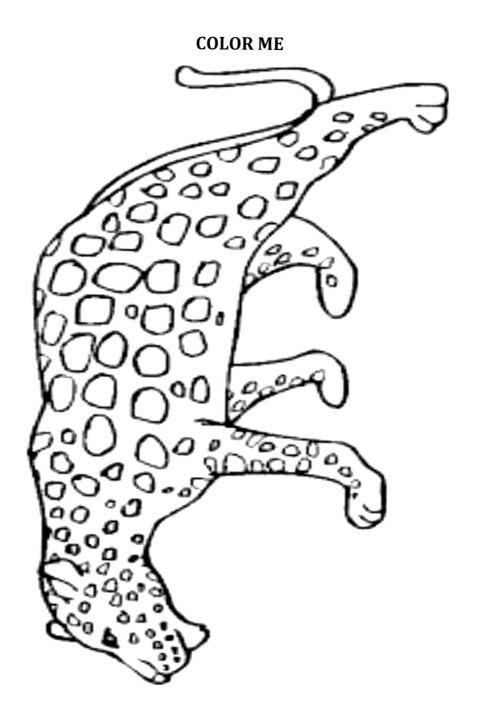

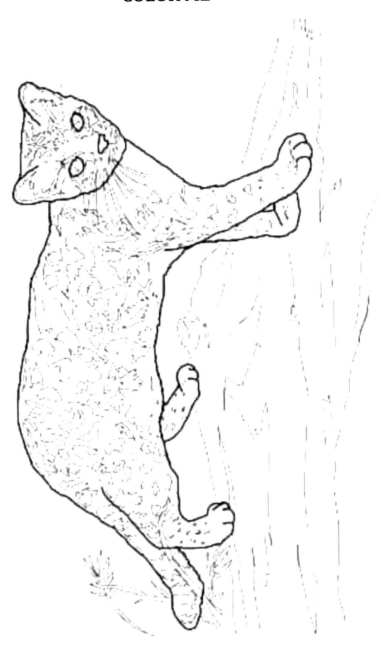

Please leave me a review here:

LisaStrattin.com/Review-Vol-323

For more Kindle Downloads Visit Lisa Strattin Author Page on Amazon Author Central

amazon.com/author/lisastrattin

To see upcoming titles, visit my website at LisaStrattin.com– most books available on Kindle!

LisaStrattin.com

FREE BOOK

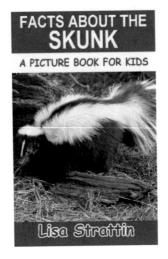

Made in the USA
Middletown, DE
26 September 2023

39454001R00024